THE QUEBEC
NEVERENDUM
COLOURING & ACTIVITY BOOK
DAVE ROSEN

VÉHICULE PRESS

For Sigrun and Rebecca

ഇൻയു

Cover art work (fairy godmother) by Dave Rosen
and Sigrun Schroeter
Special assistance by J.W. Stewart
Imaging by Simon Garamond
Printing by Imprimerie d'Édition Marquis Ltée

Special thanks to Josh Freed who coined
"Neverendum Referendum," a phrase forever etched
in the consciousness of Canadians.

Copyright © Dave Rosen 1996. All rights reserved.
Dépôt légal, Bibliothèque nationale du Québec and
the National Library of Canada, fourth quarter 1996.

CANADIAN CATALOGUING IN PUBLICATION DATA
Rosen, Dave
The Quebec Neverendum colouring and activity book
ISBN 1-55065-083-1

1. Quebec (Province)--History--Autonomy and independence
movements--Caricatures and cartoons.
2. Quebec (Province)--History--Autonomy and independence
movements--Humor. 3. Canada--Politics and
government--Caricatures and cartoons. 4. Quebec
(Province)--Politics and government--Caricatures and
cartoons. 5. Canada--Politics and government--Humor.
6. Quebec (Province)--Politics and government--Humor.
7. Canadian wit and humor, Pictorial. I. Title.

FC2926.9.R4R67 1966   971.4'04   C96-990089-9
F1053.2R67 1966

Published by Véhicule Press, P.O.B. 125, Place du Parc Station,
Montreal, Quebec H2W 1M4   (514) 844-6073
E-mail: vpress@cam.org   Web: http://www.cam.org/~vpress

Distributed by GDS, 30 Lesmill Rd., Don Mills, Ontario M3B 2T6

Printed in Canada on alkaline paper.

HOW TO USE THIS BOOK

Hello. Bonjour. How's it goin' eh?

Welcome to the **Quebec Neverendum Colouring and Activity** Book.

If you are using a touchtone phone, press "1" now. If you are not using a touchtone phone, hang up immediately and move to Winnipeg.

(Pour service en français, faites le "oui.")

Do not attempt to use this book while sleeping or watching The National. Wear a helmet and knee pads at all times. The author will not be held responsible for injuries or loss of income suffered in the course of operating this book.

IN THE EVENT OF AN EMERGENCY

If you are a federalist:
1. Roll up the book.
2. Place it to your eye. (The other way, stupid.)
3. Scan the horizon for solutions. Repeat for 129 years.

If you are a sovereignist:
1. Roll up the book.
2. Take a running start.
3. Thwack the federalist upside the head. Repeat for 129 years.

IN THE EVENT OF A REFERENDUM

You all know what to do.

CAST OF CHARACTERS

☞**Beaudoin, Louise:** PQ language minister with special responsibility for scaring Anglos. Mick Jagger look-alike.

☞**Bertrand, Guy:** Former PQ leadership candidate turned crusading federalist lawyer. His head is in his briefs.

☞**Bouchard, Lucien:** Former Canadian ambassador to France, former Tory cabinet minister, former leader of Her Majesty's Loyal Opposition, current secessionist premier of Quebec. Canada...the Land of Opportunity!

☞**Chrétien, Jean:** Canada's prime minister. He has a plan in the event Quebec declares independence...now wait a minute, it was here somewhere...maybe in that other pair of pants in the laundry hamper...Aline!

☞**Galganov, Howard:** English rights activist. Campaigned successfully for the right to see the words "jockey shorts" on a sign at Sears.

☞**Johnson, Daniel:** Quebec Liberal leader, missing in action.

☞**Landry, Bernard:** PQ finance minister and meteorologist. Likes chatting up immigrant hotel employees.

☞**Manning, Preston:** Cartoon-voiced spokesperson for Western alienation. Thinks Quebec should remain part of the country. Won't say which country.

☞**Mulroney, Brian:** The best friend Lucien Bouchard ever had.

☞**Parizeau, Jacques:** Former Quebec premier, now retired, seeks fat pension, ethnic food. Available for service club luncheons.

☞**Rhéaume, Gilles:** Sovereignist language clown, too funny for Cirque du soleil. If he didn't exist, we'd have to make him up.

IF CANADA WERE A PERSON

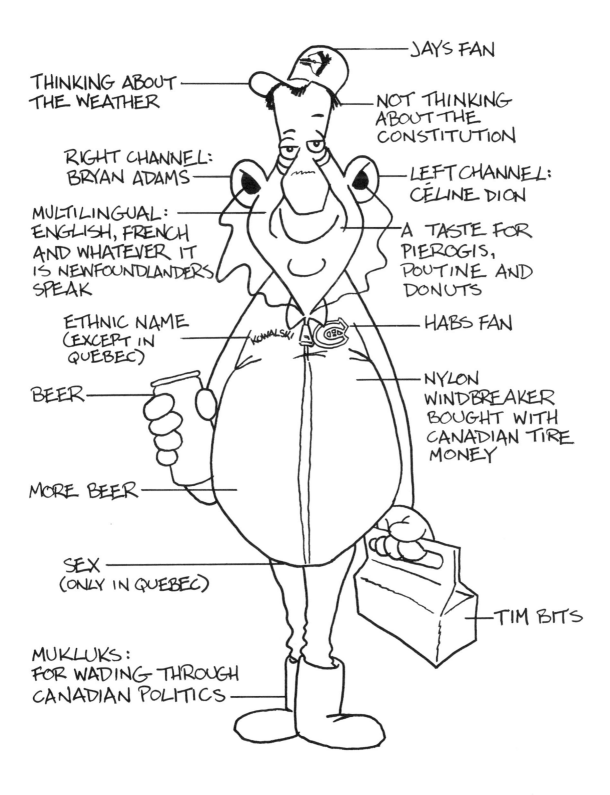

MAKE YOUR OWN MAGIC WAND

Cut out one of the symbols below. Tape it to a stick.
Now you too, just like Lucien Bouchard, are ready to
wave the magic wand of sovereignty to solve all of
Quebec's problems!

BUILD A DANIEL JOHNSON PUPPET

You will need: cardboard, string, paper fasteners,
scissors, glue, popsicle sticks

Directions:
1. Colour federalist red or nationalist
   blue, depending on day of the week or mood.
2. Cut out and glue to cardboard. Stick
   between a rock and a hard place.
3. Attach body parts with fasteners.
4. Tie to popsicle stick with string.
5. Make him dance or hang him up and leave
   him to twist in the wind!

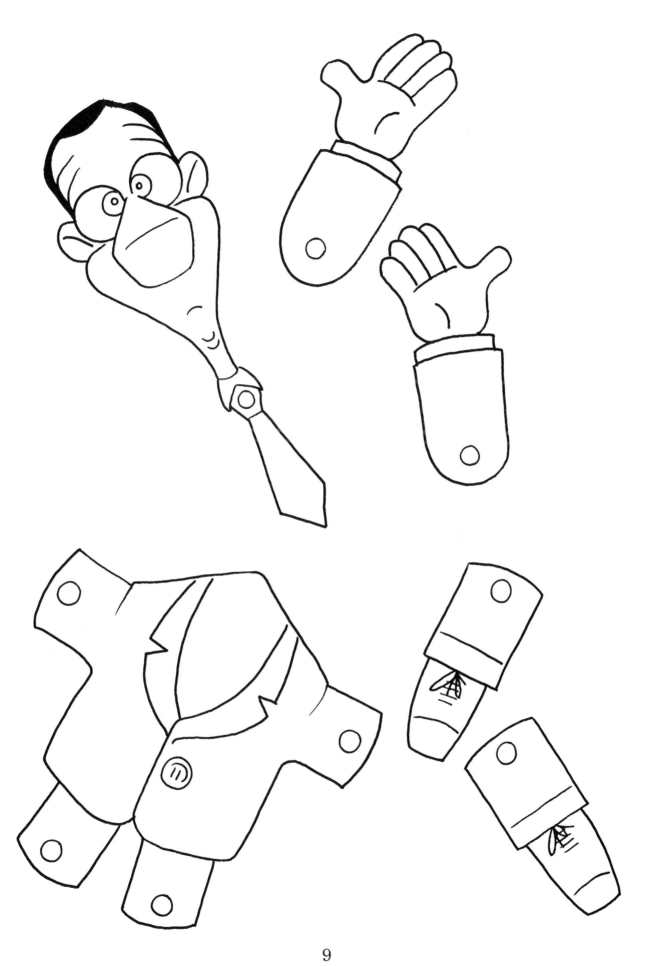

CANADA: THE POLITICAL MAP

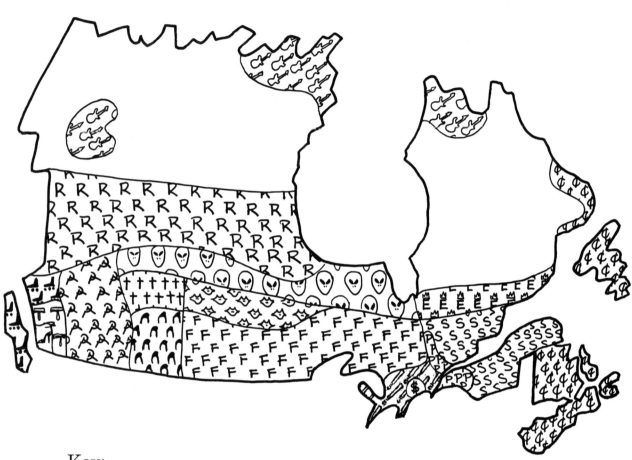

Key:

F	Federalists	†	Bible Belt	🎸	Heavy Metal Fans
S	Sovereignists	❖	Mary Kay Belt	Ẽ	Elvis Sighters
R	Reformers	⋒	Bad Haircuts	👽	Alien Abductees
P	Partitionists	⊤	Squeegee Punks	$	Rich Bastards
A	Socialists	⬧	Rollerbladers	¢	Poor Souls
✎	Teamsters	👠	Drag Queens		Empty Space

SMOKED MEAT MAZE

It's after the next referendum. The majority of Quebeckers voted
"Yes" but the West Island has split away to remain part of Canada.
The only trouble is you've got a hankering for a smoked meat sand-
wich and Schwartz's is on the other side of the wall!
How long will it take you to tunnel from your Beaconsfield bunga-
low to the Main for a taste of a lean on rye with a dill on the side?

HOW TO DRAW THE PRIME MINISTER OF CANADA

1.

2.

3.

4.

5.

6.

WORD GAME

Blacken all the squares below except those marked with a dot to find out which issue most concerns constitutional lawyers.

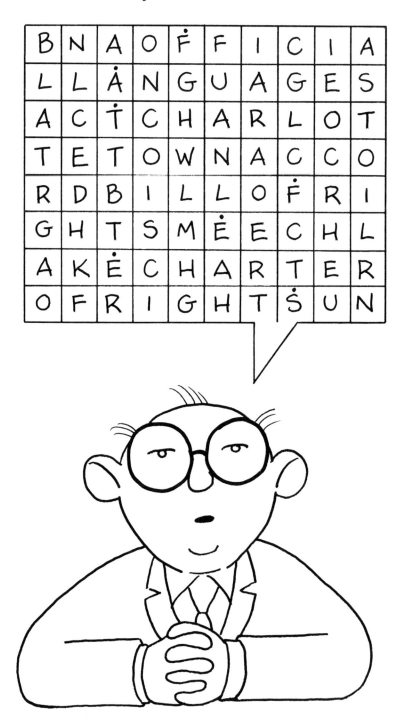

B	N	A	O	F	F	I	C	I	A
L	L	A	N	G	U	A	G	E	S
A	C	T	C	H	A	R	L	O	T
T	E	T	O	W	N	A	C	C	O
R	D	B	I	L	L	O	F	R	I
G	H	T	S	M	E	E	C	H	L
A	K	E	C	H	A	R	T	E	R
O	F	R	I	G	H	T	S	U	N

16

COLOUR-BY-NUMBERS

Depending on your politics, crayon in the nationalist image below with the colours indicated by number under the appropriate heading.

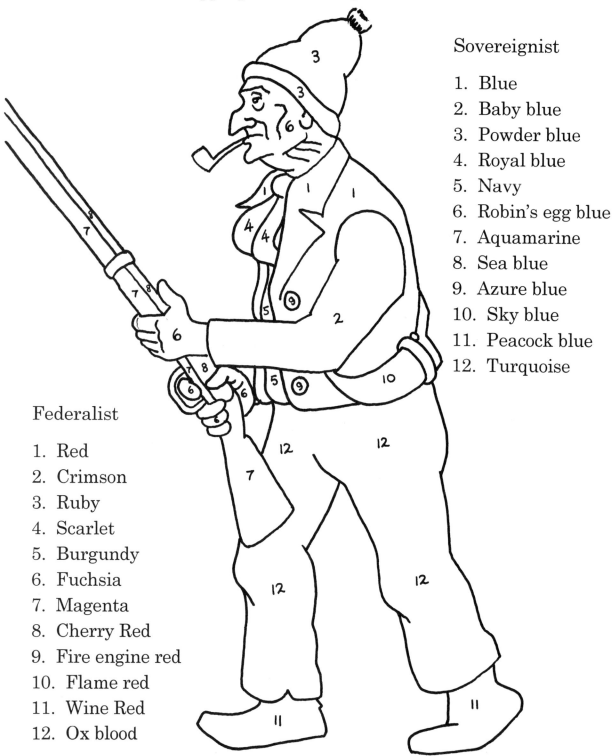

Sovereignist

1. Blue
2. Baby blue
3. Powder blue
4. Royal blue
5. Navy
6. Robin's egg blue
7. Aquamarine
8. Sea blue
9. Azure blue
10. Sky blue
11. Peacock blue
12. Turquoise

Federalist

1. Red
2. Crimson
3. Ruby
4. Scarlet
5. Burgundy
6. Fuchsia
7. Magenta
8. Cherry Red
9. Fire engine red
10. Flame red
11. Wine Red
12. Ox blood

Help Lucien decide who he wants to be today. Cut him out and dress him in the costumes provided. Fold the tabs to attach the clothes, including headgear. Voila! He's ready for another day as a man of destiny.

PAPER DOLL FUN!

PENCIL TOPPERS

Colour the faces, cut them out and tape them to the top of your pencils. Now stage your own constitutional crises!

DANIEL

LUCIEN

PRESTON

JEAN

CONNECT THE DOTS

Every few years a ghost arises from the netherworld to haunt federalist and sovereignist alike. Connect the dots and rearrange the letters below to identify the troublesome poltergeist.

A R D T U E U :_ _ _ _ _ _ _

CANADA: THE FLOW CHART

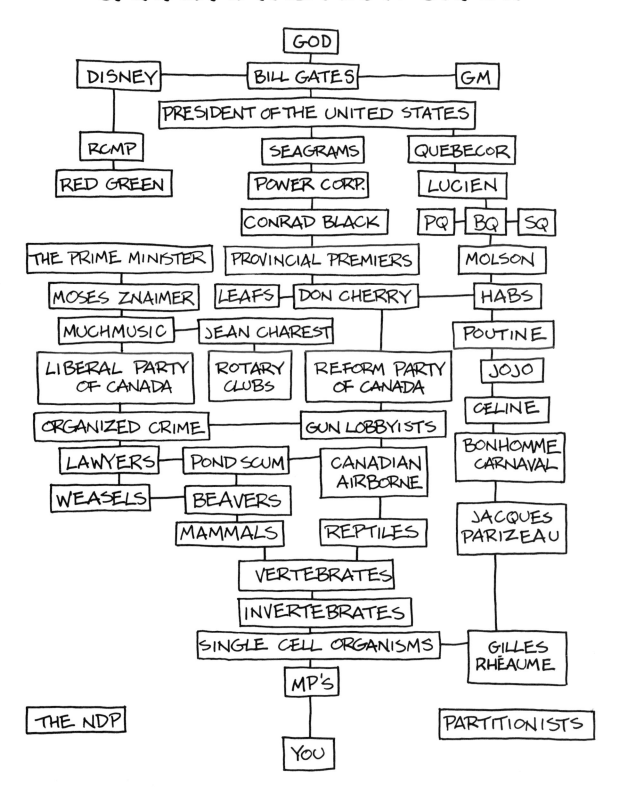

FROM THE BOOKSHELF OF LUCIEN BOUCHARD

In the top row are three of Lucien's favourite books.
Can you name three others?

THE MAN WHO WOULD BE KING

THE MOUSE THAT ROARED

GREAT EXPECTATIONS

TWO SOLITUDES
WRAPPING PAPER

Cut out the design below. Colour it in and use it to wrap a gift to a federalist.

TWO SOLITUDES
WRAPPING PAPER

Cut out the design below. Colour it in and use it to wrap a gift to a sovereignist...or a federalist.

HOW TO DRAW THE PREMIER OF QUEBEC

PRESTON MASK

Cut this page out and glue it to a piece of cardboard. Punch out the eye holes. Punch out and run string through the ear holes. Tie the mask behind your head and practice speaking high school French in a crystal-shattering whine until Quebec leaves the country.

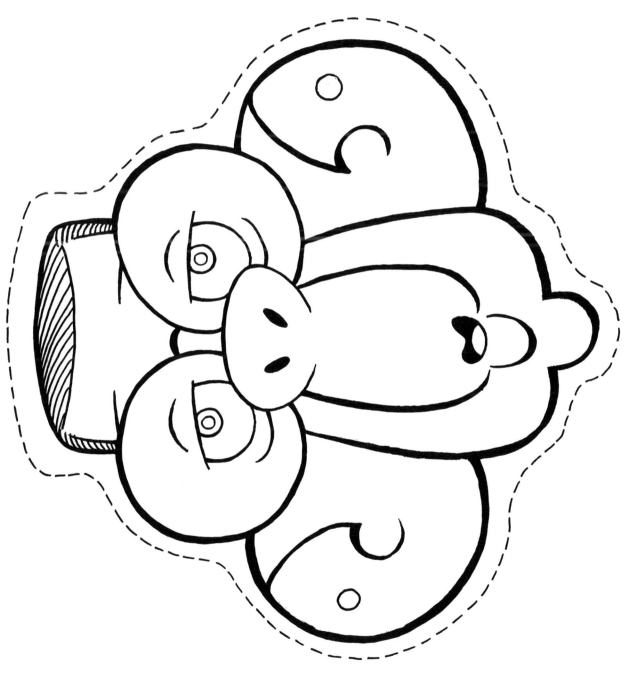

ANAGRAMS

Rearrange the letters in the word "sovereignty"
to reveal at least six hidden messages.

1. _____

2. _____

3. _____

4. _____

5. _____

6. _____

HOW TO TALK TO ANGLOS

1. Sound vaguely apologetic.

2. Make colourful ethnic references.

3. Stroke your audience.

4. Always finish with a joke.

After a trip to Montreal, this Western Canadian finally understands that Quebec's distinctiveness resides in its:

a. language
b. vibrant culture
c. joie de vivre
d. lax liquor laws

MORE ANAGRAMS

How many additional words or phrases can you create by rearranging the following names?

Guy Bertrand: Drab grey nut

                  _____

                  _____

                  _____

Gilles Rhéaume: He is large mule

                  _____

                  _____

                  _____

Howard Galganov: Avow hog lard nag

                  _____

                  _____

                  _____

Pierre Bourgault: Our pet rug be liar

                  _____

                  _____

                  _____

Sheila Copps: She is cop pal

                  _____

                  _____

                  _____

Bernard Landry: Darn Dr. Blarney

                  _____

                  _____

                  _____

JEAN "SPACEMAN" CHRETIEN

OTTAWA Dodgers

LEGENDS OF SPORT NO.1

CONNECT THE DOTS

Connect the dots in the drawing below to show who is looking over Lucien's shoulder.

Ripoff's ~ Believe It or Else!

IN 1759, FRENCH GENERAL MONTCALM AND ENGLISH GENERAL WOLFE WERE BOTH MORTALLY WOUNDED AND DIED ON THE PLAINS OF ABRAHAM AT THE BATTLE OF QUEBEC, SETTING OFF 250 YEARS OF BITTER SQUABBLING OVER QUEBEC'S PLACE IN CANADA.

IN 1996, THE DIRECT DESCENDANTS OF THE TWO MEN MET AND SHOOK HANDS, ALSO ON THE PLAINS OF ABRAHAM, *BUT NOBODY NOTICED!*

IT IS ESTIMATED THAT A *SINGLE* BOX OF MATZOH WITH AN ENGLISH LABEL ON IT CAN RAISE THE BLOOD PRESSURE OF 10,000 SOVEREIGNISTS!

MATZOHS KOSHER FOR PASSOVER

AS A CUB SCOUT, *LUCIEN BOUCHARD* ONCE EARNED A MERIT BADGE FOR CARVING A BUST OF MACKENZIE KING ENTIRELY OUT OF *MARGARINE!*

HOW TO COUNT VOTES IN QUEBEC

1. Separate the "yes" ballots from the "no" ballots.
2. Count the "yes" ballots.
3. Place the "yes" votes in container A.
4. Place the "no" votes in container B.

FROM THE VCR OF JEAN CHRETIEN

In the top row are three of the PM's favourite movies.
Can you name three others?

NO-D CONSTITUTIONAL GLASSES

You're a provincial premier and you want to see a solution to the constitutional conundrum (work with me here).

Cut out the "No-D" constitutional glasses below. Do not cut holes in the lenses. Now put them on.

What do you see?

Exactly.

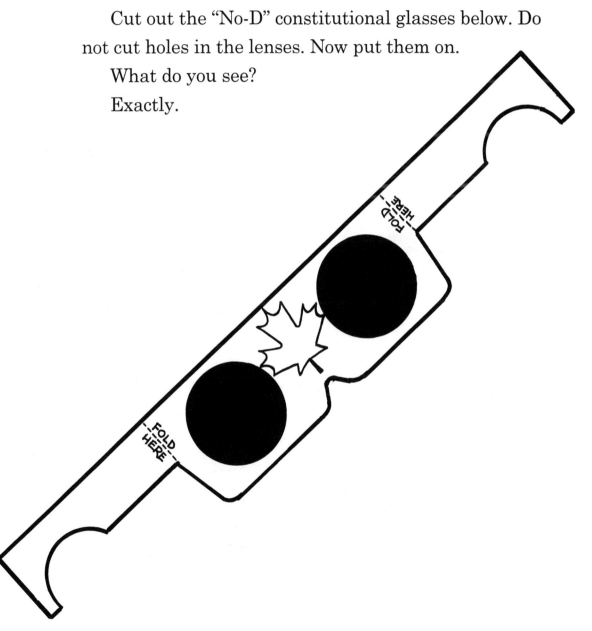

LUCIEN BOUCHARD'S TOP TEN REASONS FOR QUEBEC TO SEPARATE

10. Canadian Tire can be renamed Pneu Québécois.

9. No more pesky flag-waving Canadians obstructing Montreal's safe and courteous motorists.

8. Cheaper housing on the West Island.

7. The poodle can replace the beaver as a national symbol.

6. Will be able to post thousands more "For Rent" and "Going-out-of-business" signs in French only.

5. No more listening to Mike Harris' golfing stories at first ministers meetings.

4. Audrey can finally tell her folks what it is her husband does for a living.

3. Can turn our attention to more serious questions, like when is Celine going to have a baby.

2. Who needs jobs anyway?

1. Just because.

T-SHIRT QUIZ

Match the T-shirts with the political preferences listed below.

Federalist ___   Partitionist ___

Sovereignist ___   Undecided ___

THE "MORDY"

Awarded each year to the anglo or ethnic Montrealer who has caused the most apoplexy among Quebec nationalists.

LEGENDS OF SPORT
NO.2

PLAN B!

After almost losing the last referendum, the federal government has finally come up with a foolproof plan for stopping Lucien Bouchard. See if you can guess what it is from the elements pictured below.

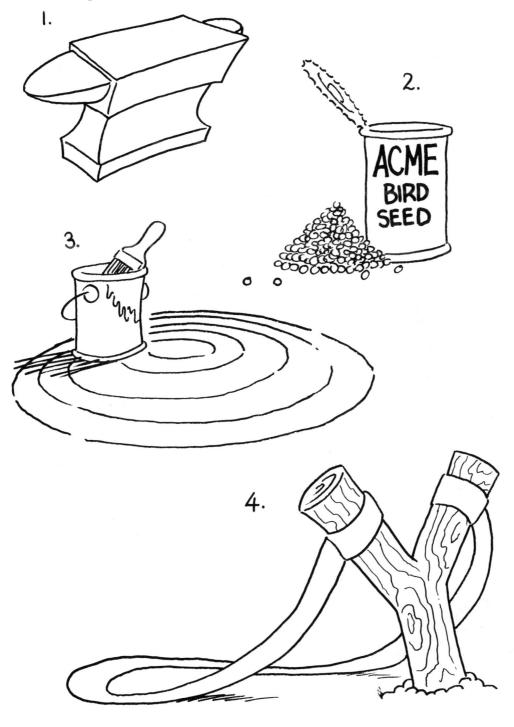

1.

2.

3.

4.

48

Lucien has two speeches to make today; one to U.S. business leaders, the other to Quebec voters. Help him write his speeches by cutting out the strips of words below. Then cut slots in the speech ballon and slide the strips through until you find the appropriate adjective.

Now guess which words are meant for the Americans and which are meant for domestic consumption.

QUEBEC IS

HUMILIATED   OUTRAGED   IMPRISONED   ENSLAVED

WARM   OPEN   VIBRANT   PROFITABLE

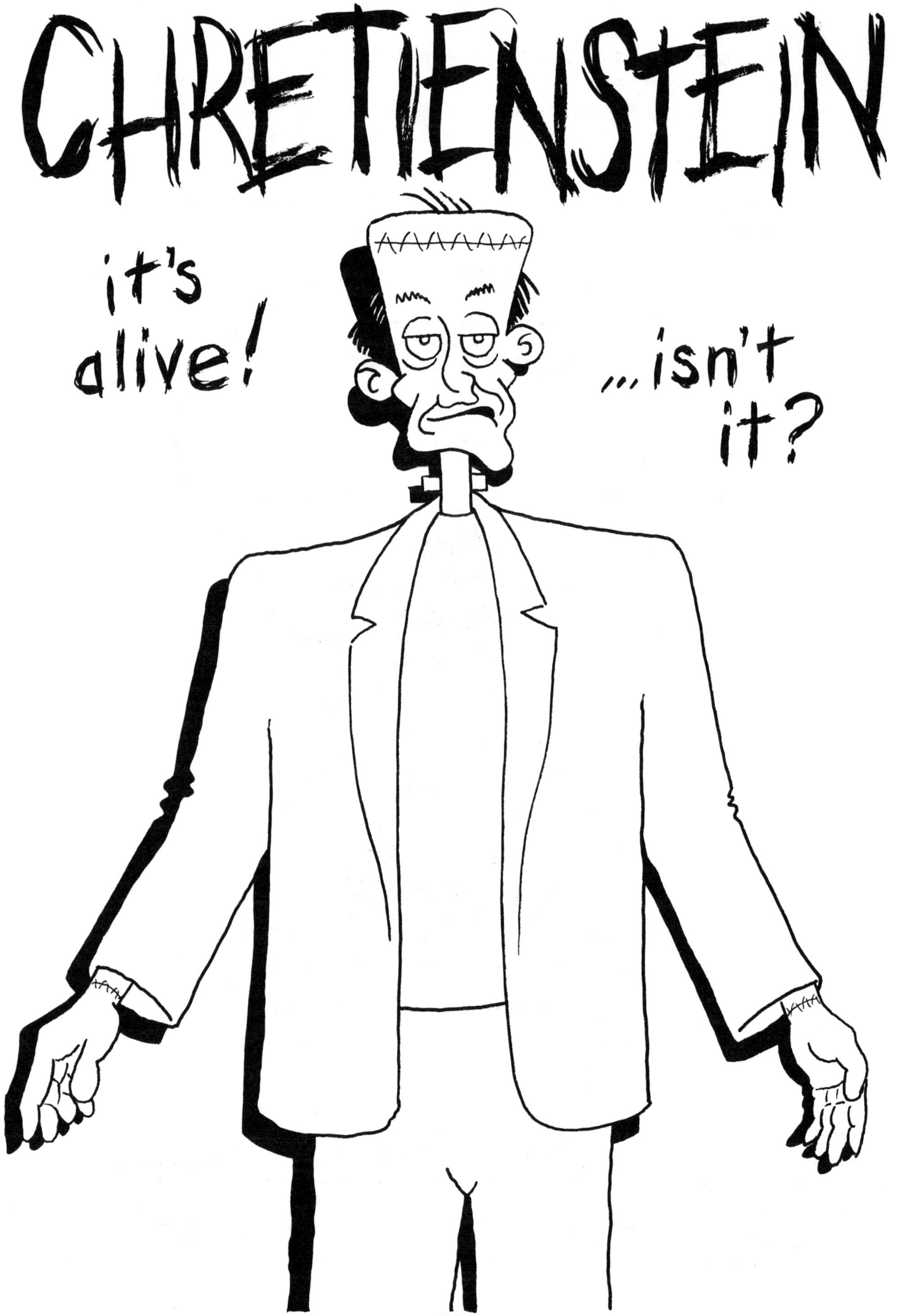
CHRETIENSTEIN
it's alive!
...isn't it?

NUMBERS GAME

You are a reporter working for the francophone media, sent to cover a massive Canadian unity rally in downtown Montreal. Would you estimate the crowd at:

a. 150,000
b. 100,000
c. 75,000
d. 35,000

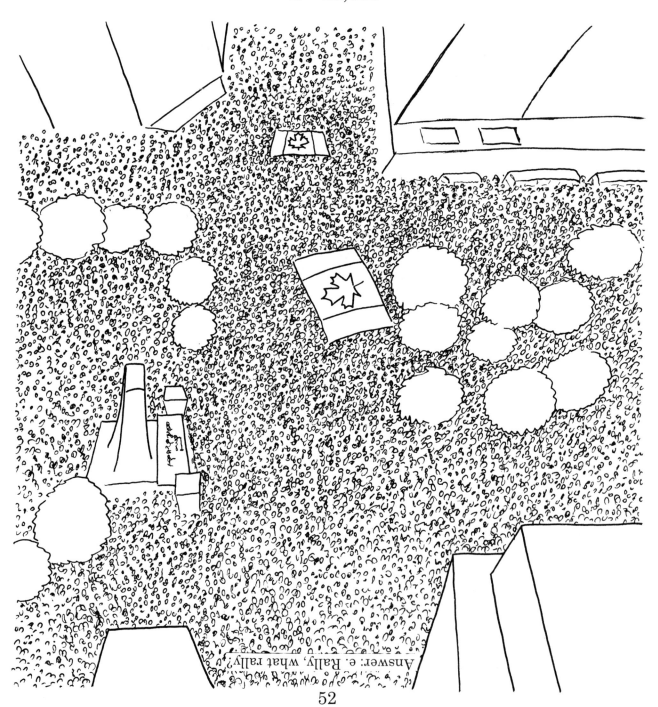

Answer: e. Rally, what rally?

WALL PUZZLE

Lucien is building a wall around Quebec. To stop him, shade in the letters that spell "Canada" on the wall. To help him, spell the word "Quebec" from the letters in the pile of bricks.

This is the prime minister. He is signing a document.
This document:

a. recognizes Quebec as a distinct society.
b. pledges no negotiations with Quebec's separatist government.
c. names Leslie Nielsen governor general.
d. orders a loaf of bread, a dozen eggs and two-four of Labatt Blue.

CONSTITUTIONAL HAIRSTYLING

Help Lucien find a new "do"!

HOW TO BUILD AN INDEPENDENT QUEBEC

You will need:

empty tissue box   construction paper
paper towel tube   scissors and glue
markers   chutzpah

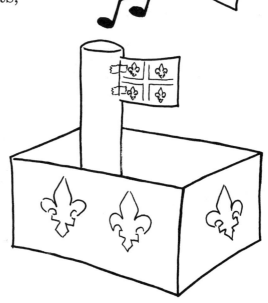

Directions:

1. With the help of a sovereignty commission, cut out one side of the box as shown.

2. Glue construction paper on all sides of box and decorate with fleurs de lys.

3. Cover the paper towel tube with more construction paper, studies, reports, and polls.

4. Cut flags from remaining paper.

5. Compose national anthem.

6. Glue flags and tube to box, declare independence.

7. Hold referendum.

8. Hold another referendum.

9. Keep holding referendums until you get a "yes" vote.

Match the political leader with the product he'd be best suited to endorse.

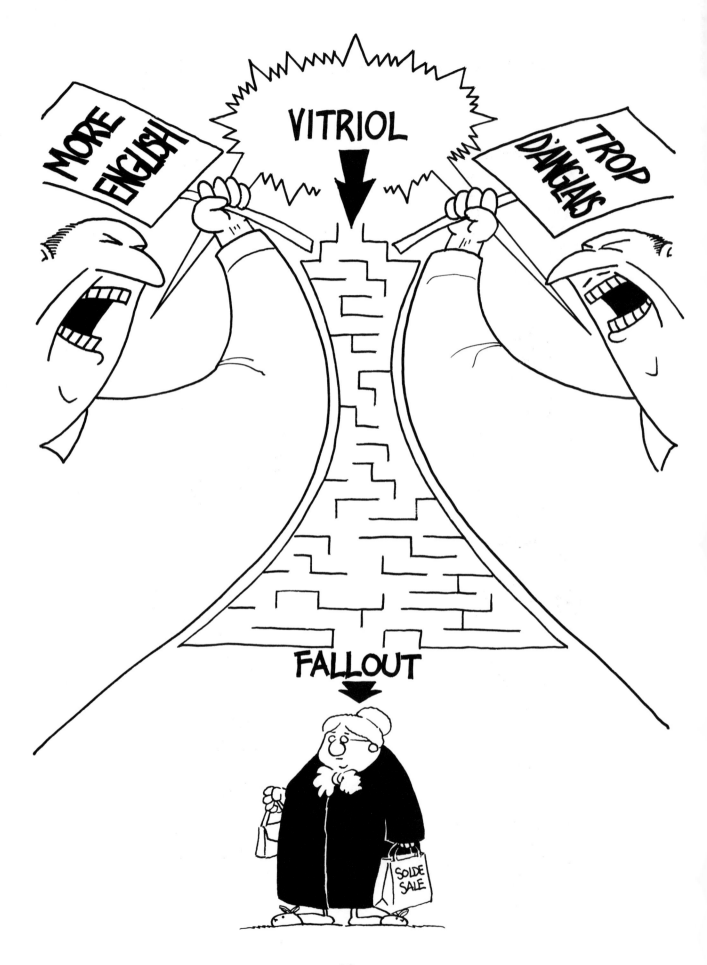

TONGUE TROOPER KIT

The Commission de protection de la langue française wants you!

    Enlist in the language police by cutting out and pinning on the badge provide below. Then cut out the ruler and you're ready to start measuring the letters on English and French signs.

    You'll have hours of fun enforcing Quebec's commercial signs law in your very own neighbourhood!

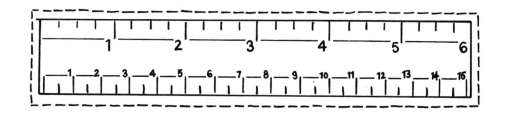

With best wishes to all my ethnic friends — Jacques

HOW QUEBEC WENT FROM
HUMILIATION to NATION

I Can Make YOU a Have-Not Nation, Too, in Only 5 Minutes!

If YOU, like Quebec, possess a false sense of injustice or suffer imagined slights, then give me just five minutes of your time. I'll transform you into a tiny, independent country that has REAL social problems!

"Linguistic Tension Does It!"

Use my patented "Linguistic Tension" method in which you blame all your troubles on "le fédéral," "les anglais," "les autres," in fact everybody except the American multinationals who own you. You'll put on attitude, increase your resentment and become embittered to the point of voting YES in the next referendum. Or the one after that.

Don't put it off! Fill out your ballot and vote YES today!